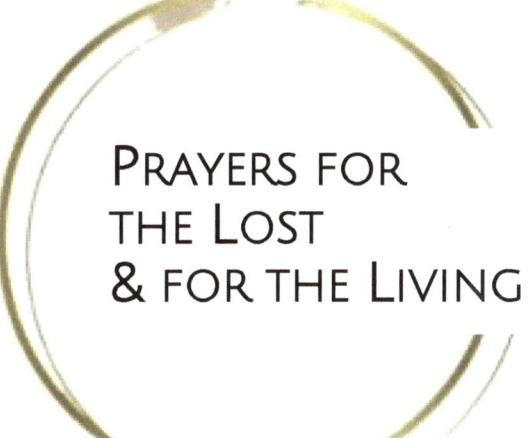

Prayers for the Lost & for the Living

ISBN: 979-8-218-61532-1

Edited by Isabelle Altman
Images and cover design by Dina Greenberg
Author's photo by Belinda Keller
Book design by Alan Abrams

Sligo Creek Publishing Co.
Silver Spring, Maryland
www.sligocreekpublishing.com

PRAYERS FOR THE LOST & FOR THE LIVING

DINA GREENBERG

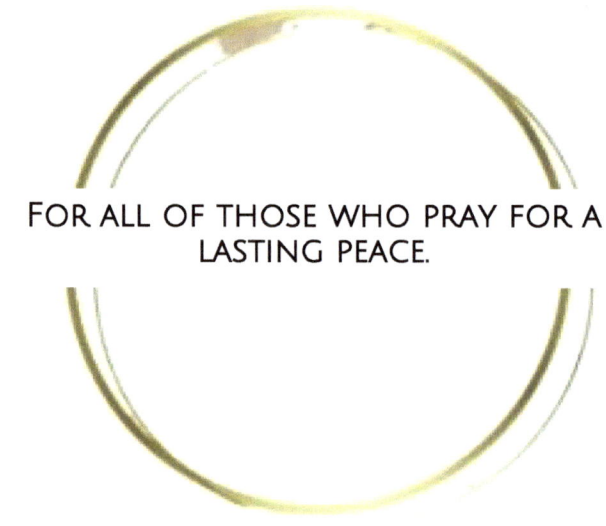

FOR ALL OF THOSE WHO PRAY FOR A
LASTING PEACE.

CONTENTS

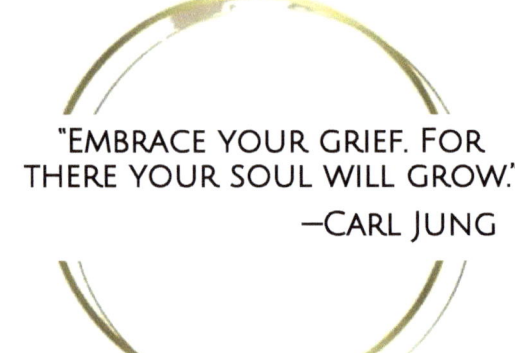

"EMBRACE YOUR GRIEF. FOR
THERE YOUR SOUL WILL GROW."
—CARL JUNG

"MAY WE ALL HOLD SORROW AND FEAR
WITH GRACE AND KEEP REACHING TOWARD
THE BEAUTY, JOY, AND
CONNECTION THAT SURROUNDS US."
—JEN JOHNSON JOHNSON, LCMHC

IN TIMES LIKE THESE

think of your spirit animal
think of a soaring eagle, forget
your chorus of tears
nights stretching aimless and fraught, slick

shrapnel of unhinged grief, then
a faith-guided missile striking its target, *think*
of a place you feel safe, think
ocean, not desert, forget

keening mothers buckled
over green-draped coffins, don't
think of martyred sons and husbands or
towers of flame, forget

armbands emblazoned with yellow stars,
bodies stacked like cordwood
and blue-inked tattoos, *We*

walk through a sun-kissed meadow, don't think
of migrant children drowning in powerful rivers,
infants crushed beneath weight of leaden skies, *Think*

of a tropical island, remember
the son of God, a Buddhist prayer wheel or
silken embers floating to earth like dust, not
human flesh, not fragments of bone
remember the Holy Land, remember
the burning bush, not
a burning cross, a burning Humvee

Think of your favorite color, think of
a blood-red kiss, not
blood-riven streets
a noose
a graveyard, remember
a purple-draped cross, forget
the bombed-silent marketplace, bodies
mounded like rotten fruit, *think*
of a prayer, say the Shema
say a dua for peace, *Remember*

a song from your childhood, never
a severed foot, rattle of bullets, children
cowered in classrooms, in piles of rubble
in theaters and shopping malls, *Think*

of a place you feel safe
a temple or a mosque, think
synagogue or church, not Shoah, not
Nakba, not War or Jihad, *and*
let us begin with ooooommmmmm

WE ARE SEEKERS

FAR FROM HOME

In a dream my mother flutters through a foreign marketplace in a city unknown but still familiar. She dashes through cobble-stoned alleyways, twirling, then ducking from sight, only to reappear, girlish laughter barely contained behind her flayed fingers. A turquoise scarf encircles her waist. Dime store bangles clatter at her wrists. Saffron-colored tights with a run the length of the Thames. Second-hand Mary Janes, the soles worn paper-thin and translucent. That black knit skirt, pilled from years of slipshod laundering. Furred by a succession of cats whose finnicky warmth my mother covets. An outrageous outfit—not so very different than the ones she's fashioned in her recent waking life. But remember the peek-a-boo dress—the one whose oval cutouts made two identical picture frames for her tanned, taut midriff? She wore that dress when I was a girl. And she wore an A-line dress then, too, of crisp, lilac poplin. My little-girl dress, an exact replica of my mother's, itchy where she'd trimmed the neckline with rickrack a darker shade of purple. In the dream I do not chase her—her movements so quick and crafty, designed to elude me. In the dream I do not tend her as she once tended me. Here, plastic tubes no longer tether my mother to this earth. Blinking machines no longer track her every heartbeat. In the dream her legs carry her wherever she pleases. In the dream I cannot hear her beg for home.

GHUSL

Soak soft cotton wool in warm water
scented with camphor and
leaves from the plum tree, turn
your beloved toward Mecca
to wash away rivers
of blood-thickened mud,

place over his lower parts
a clean white cloth. And
press a wad of cotton firmly
where each bullet entered.

Gently wash where the flesh has
burned from his face,
then the right arm
and then the left

wash the right hand, next the left,
make clean the torso
where the bruises go purple and ochre
like the late autumn harvest,

cleanse the abdomen
thighs and shins
the right foot only
for the left you could not salvage,

wash three or five or seven times
wrap your beloved in the clean white *kafan*
his mother stitched, release
your beloved from your embrace and
spill to the earth the sullied waters, release
your tears in praise and sorrow.

GHUSL

STRONG SWIMMER

On Dec. 10 and 16, 1941, the Ustaše, *Yugoslavia's Nazi regime, imprisoned, tortured, and then murdered 350 Jews in the city of Brčko, Bosnia. This poem bears witness to each of the souls who perished here.*

I imagine a young woman. She is tall and slim. Her dark brown hair falls gently to her shoulders. The woman's eyes are blue and she shields them for a few moments from the sunlight—aligning her right hand to her forehead like a visor. Let's say this young woman—a woman not far beyond her girlhood—is Jewish. This woman is not me, but she could be me, even though my eyes are brown. Let's say her name is Mariška and she plans to become a doctor one day in Vienna, the city of her birth. This young woman is not me. I have none of the requisite scientific aptitude to become a doctor. But let's say that Mariška's father is a doctor, a surgeon. She idolizes him. The woman is not me. I did not idolize my father, though I loved him. Let's say that it's 1938 and a man named Hitler is keen on killing Jews. In Austria, this fever dream is born. So, now, Mariška and her parents are in Brčko, a city in Bosnia where the river Sava runs beneath an iron bridge. Let's say it's 1941 and other—similar—monsters are keen on killing Jews and Serbs alike here. Let's say that Mariška's hands are bound with wire, that she casts her eyes downward to the bottle-green water as it rushes madly beneath the iron bridge. The river is crystalline and wild. Or it is placid and meager. Perhaps her right hand does not form a visor. Perhaps her eyes are not blue. The woman is not me, but she could be me. The woman is a strong swimmer, something I am not. Let's say the *Ustaša* carry out Hitler's savage deeds throughout the entire Kingdom of Yugoslavia, but in Brčko this work is especially precise and thorough. Perhaps one day in December, two-hundred Jews in Brčko are beaten with sledgehammers and scythes. They are slashed with knives and axes. They are bound with wire. They are shoved over the iron railing and into the water below, blood from their wounds the color of rust. This is not my blood but it could be. Let's say that several days later, the *Ustaše* complete their task. Now another one-hundred-and-fifty Jews are bound and beaten and drowned. Or perhaps they are buried alive in deep pits, their screams silenced by earth the color of shit. Or perhaps this is, in fact, what fills the pits.

Let's say Mariška's fate belongs to the first group. Perhaps she is a strong swimmer. Perhaps she Houdini-s her hands free from their wired cage. Perhaps her strokes are long and graceful and powerful and when she raises her head from the water to draw a breath she prays her parents are alive. This woman is not me but she could be. I am not a strong swimmer but perhaps I could be. I rarely pray but perhaps I will begin.

TREE OF LIFE

AFTER FLORENCE, ROOFTOP STIGMATA

i
Blue tarps are our tell tale
rooftop stigmata
some with
some without
relief   belief   blessings
after Florence
tribes emerge
survivors   first responders
haves   have-nots

evacuees exiled still
the city   an island
entombed in darkness
while the heavens pour
unrelenting
for days

brackish water laps and lashes
fetid   dark
bloating rivers   and creeks   streets
ruthless trespass
          eddies
through houses and churches and barns
water   water
seeps and sifts   remains
of chickens   pigs
family photos
kindergarten plaster-of-Paris
treasures
and those
too poor to leave
stay
supplicants   weary   defeated   hopeful
faithful

diehards
those with means
those without
hunkered down inside
sodden drywall and timbers
shamed   defiant   fearful
penitent
factions
separated by   grace
by income
by race

believers and sinners
battered or spared
by wind sheer
high tides   and storm surge
random or divine
rooftops
lives   livelihoods
unmoored
or   Saved
spared
or crushed
beneath the weight
of thick ancient oaks

on dirt roads
tin-can trailers
tossed into ditches and fields
their occupants
forgotten
forsaken   still
and again

ii
weeks later
mold spreads feathery dark fingers
inside closets and cupboards
creeps beneath floorboards
while fans roar and roar
their demon mouths agape

in the city
flotsam lurks at curbside
sodden mattresses   sofas   carpets
shards of window glass
strips of aluminum   coiled like serpents
clapboard blackened and   rotting
laden   soiled

but in the next zip code
private haulers whisk away
neatly bundled branches
from quiet cul-de-sacs
on HOA trash days
Mexican gardeners arrive
by the truckload
cleansed-again   swimming pools
shimmer aqua-blue
and

in high school gymnasiums
the poorest still sleep head-to-head
on FEMA cots   kneel
in prayer
sweat   shiver
under tin-foil blankets they subsist on MREs
bottled water
donated canned goods while   of course

good works abound
they rush and swell like cresting rivers
southbound
good souls minister
to those less fortunate
they bail   and bail and bail
buckets of tears
buckets of sorrow older than Noah's
          always   always
they cast their eyes to God
to the blue-tarped heavens
they pray   and pray   and pray

until the next one comes

NOT OURS

Sleek white hull parts the sea like Moses but the boy still daydreams his six-year-old boy dreams. Spindly arms and legs singed vacation-pink and fleeced with the same flaxen hair of his eyebrows. Lashes and buzz-cut bleached white in the sun. Wake from the speedboat slaps harder against his family's rented skiff. The boy's feet slip, the small O of his mouth when his skull hits the cleat, and he is tumbling, tumbling, the sea slapping harder. He thrashes, but those angry blue-gray waves spread out forever, so he opens his mouth wider to call out to his parents and the ocean fills him.

ii

A Coast Guard helicopter cleaves the August haze of saltmarsh while pleasure craft still bob on the sound. At the dock, mothers and fathers gaze up to postcard-blue sky, air heavy as a womb, scent of pines and sand, harbinger of copter blades—and dread lodges deep in their throats, in their bellies. *Did you hear? A little boy's gone missing.*

iii

Tendrils of sea grass worry his sunburned limbs, brackish waves lapping the shore when they lift him from the waters—no woven basket of reeds, no surreptitious palace adoption, just plastic bottles and cigarette butts. Later, the stricken bob their heads. *Yes.* Islanded in grief, the parents shake and sob and blame, lassitude thick and murky as the swill where the current dragged their boy. They can't help but hear the others pray: *Not ours, not ours, not ours.*

PEACE

SETTING ANCHOR

Ivy hears the thunder, how it curls up and over itself, ebbing and churning and folding. A low rumble at first, but now she feels the storm gathering power, its timbre a growing weight in the pit of her stomach. The weight is familiar. Kneeling to reach into Rocco's doggy bed, Ivy winces. Her bones crackle and she imagines her own demise not so far behind their sweet pet.

Wrapped in a cashmere shawl Ivy hopes Celia won't miss, the little Yorkie lies still against her thrumming heart. She rocks him in her arms as a mother would her baby, grateful that Celia is visiting her niece for the weekend. No chance for her to coax Ivy off her course. After thirty years, Ivy knows Celia's ways.

At the boat launch, chop slaps against the bulkhead. The skiff groans on its tethers. Ivy takes small, careful steps, the dry bag slung over her shoulder and Rocco inside her canvas tote. As the dock shifts beneath her, Ivy unwinds the rain-slick lines from their cleats. A jagged streak of lightning shears the moonless sky; thunder-deaf, Ivy clambers aboard.

Even at low throttle, she sees the ghost-white phosphorescence as the hull parts the storm-chopped waves. Ivy remembers a time with her father at the fishing pier. A passing pleasure boat trailing its gleaming wake. At nine, she believed her father had conjured this magic for her alone.

She pilots the skiff into the last cut, cord grass tunneled and vividly green as her beacon sweeps the bend. Ahead lies the spit of land she's never once located without Celia's instructions. Until now.

Just off-shore, Ivy kills the engine and sets the anchor. The rain's turned chilly. Muck-and-salt-tasting in the wind. Her bare legs sting, chalky-pale as the sand dollars she and Celia collect here each summer. The hull sways and rocks. Ivy hears her father's words. Familiar. Daggers fueled first by fury or disappointment, then finally a profound and relentless disgust that barred Ivy from her childhood home, from her family. Even from the long months of her father's dying.

She lifts the tote, Rocco no heavier than the spare sweatshirt and shorts folded neatly inside the dry bag. Ivy scoots her bottom across the bow, holding the tote aloft, and slips her sandal-clad feet into the water. Brackish waves lap at her thighs as she wades to shore.

The soil beneath the banyans is heavier than Ivy would have expected—so many years since she's hauled buckets of mud from the ocean to dribble sandcastles as her parents looked on. Ivy digs with the spade she's pulled from the dry bag, and when the grave is deep, as deep as she imagines a grave must be, she places Rocco inside, the cashmere shawl now a proper shroud.

Finally, Ivy's flashlight beam haloes the gravesite, a slight mound with three sand dollars pressed tenderly at the center. Kneeling, she extracts her childhood Bible. "The Lord is my shepherd," she begins.

PRAYER FOR A PANDEMIC

Awaken at two a.m.
day four of Passover, Easter Sunday
enumerate the dead &
the afflicted
break open your heart again
don't fight
the pounding fear
growing there, relinquish
each footfall, touch
silken ash to forehead
make the sign of the cross

Believe, believe
behold the Paschal Lamb
behold the promised land
face the east
rock from heel to toe
drop and give me twenty
repent, repent
kiss the ring
click your heels together & say
God is great, God is good

Cover your head with a *mitpachat*
cover your face with a homemade mask
sneeze into your elbow
press your hand to your heart
breathe in through your nose
& out through your mouth
surrender, say the Pledge
of Allegiance, kneel
open your mouth
for the wafer

Make an inventory of all parts
before you begin assembly
enumerate the dead &
the afflicted

rinse & repeat
break your heart wide open
don't think the unthinkable
don't think, don't think
when thoughts drift in
acknowledge them without judgement

Wander through another day
like a ghost, say
the *Shema*, say *Kaddish*
praise *Allah*, press
your forehead to the earth
awaken at two a.m.

enumerate the dead &
the afflicted
break your heart wide open
don't fight
the pounding fear
growing there, acknowledge sorrow
without judgment
don't think, don't think
don't think the unthinkable
awaken at two a.m.

GRACE

BOY, BEARING

i.

I picture you hunched at your desk, a college boy now, but slight as
you were at ten. Then, you wielded a plastic light saber, slashed at the
air, already whirling into shadow. Now, only your ear buds divine the
faint beating of your heart. Now, a plastic fork your weapon of
choice: tracing endless patterns on your plate—circling and
dividing—debating. Refusing or purging.

ii

Your face is paler these days, unshaved and hollow—a palimpsest of
the plump-cheeked boy I once held. Then, your sweet lips poised and
expectant; head tipped back for that first trickle of something holy.
Pure.

iii

Your parents named you Christopher, after the saint. A dutiful boy
and true to your namesake, you struggled beneath the weight of Him
from the start. Year after year, wading through depths of sorrow.
Now, you weigh and measure each morsel. Each sip, and breath, and
sin. And still the river thirsts for you. You for it. Weary, you tread
and tread and tread, bearing your slow and constant penance.

ALL THAT WE HEAR EN LOS ESTADOS UNIDOS

Ellos dicen: *Ve a dormir!*
        You tremble.
Tú preguntas: *¿Qué es este lugar?*
Their eyes tell you nothing.
Tú recuerdas tu madre siempre decía: *Dulces sueños, niñito.*
        You try to remember her face.
Tú preguntas *¿Cuándo volverá mi madre?*
        They say: Soon. They say: *Pronto.*
Ellos dicen: *¡Para de llorar!* Cry baby!
        Your tears flow like the river from which they
dragged her.
Ellos dicen: *¡Silencio!*
        Your small heart leaps with fear.
Ellos preguntan: *¿Te gusta* ice cream? *¿Te gusta* Coca Cola?
¿Te gusta chicken nuggets?
        Your stomach churns with hunger.
Tú dices: No. *No tengo hambre.*
        You remember her hand on your cheek *como una
bendición del sacerdote.*
Tú preguntas: *¿Cuándo volverá mi madre?*
They say: Soon. They say: *Pronto.*

LOS MILAGROS

Rosaria is afraid that she will die before her granddaughter is born. Luz and Umberto have told her that their next child will be a girl because the American doctor has shown them the little square of plastic film—a ghostly form swimming against the darkness like starlight—a picture, the doctor says, of the daughter still forming inside of Luz's belly. This, Rosaria knows, is unreliable, so here among the candles flickering inside blue glass and wisps of musky incense, Rosaria prays to *La Virgen de Guadalupe*. Above the plastic altar that she carried here from Mexico, Rosaria has pinned the tiny medal of *La Niña*, along with a short prayer that she has written on a scrap of paper.

Here in America, she lives in a narrow room with Gabriella, her seventh grandchild, not including the one that is on the way. In the house she shares with Luz and Umberto, Ricarda, Miguel, and little Gabriella, Rosaria has lined a drawer with pink paper that smells like powder. She's filled it with tiny sweaters and leggings that she crocheted, pearl pink, the yarn so soft and fine she had to rip out countless rows and begin again. *Limpia*, Rosaria thought then. Much better to start fresh than to carry your mistakes with you any further.

Now the drawer is full, and Luz's belly keeps her from seeing her toes. Rosaria is washing this youngest daughter's hair, rich brown like mushroom soil. Rosaria feels old when she leans over to rinse out the shampoo. For a moment she is afraid. She is weak and fights for air. Then the moment passes. Her daughter's dark hair glows like something holy as it spreads across her shoulders. Rosaria rubs almond oil into Luz's scalp. From the kitchen with its one small window, Rosaria looks out onto the single row of trailers where families huddle, holding on to what they remember. Again, her heart beats frantically, like a blackbird's wings against window glass. Then the moment goes dark.

In the hospital room with its hissing and blinking machines, with its pale green walls, and the city's wailing sirens that grow louder in the night, Rosaria has placed a small soapstone statue of *La Virgen* on the bedside table. Now her prayers will still be heard, even though she is so far away from Mexico and from the church. From where *El Niño Fidencio*, *Santo Niño de Atocha*, *Santa Lucía*, and *Don Predrito Jaramillo* were all so close she could touch them.

The doctor's brisk words rouse Rosaria from rest. A nurse hurries from the room. A curtain whisks along its metal tracks. A tall man—neither young nor old—wears a white coat with red looping script. He studies a sheaf of papers as he stands before Rosaria's bed. These are the papers upon which the other doctors have written their secrets. Rosaria looks down at her hands, creased like baked earth. She looks down at the place where the needle is taped. The medicine drips from a clear bag that hangs from a tall pole, and into a little plastic tube that sometimes one nurse, and sometimes another, slides onto the needle.

She does not look into the American doctor's eyes. She is afraid that he can see deep inside her, that he, too, knows why she has gotten sick, that he will not want to waste his powerful American medicine on an old woman like herself. She has already written to her sister Catalina, asked her to please send the herbs that *la curandera* crushes and boils and strains into medicine that she will drink quickly, swallowing the bitter taste like a penance.

The tall doctor is speaking again. He grasps Rosaria's wrist, bruised where the nurses have pierced her skin with needles to fill long glass tubes with *sangre*, scarlet-purple, for the doctors to study. This doctor's words frighten Rosaria. He looks only at the papers. He scribbles down his own secrets and walks quickly away, already talking into the little telephone he produces from the folds of his crisp white coat.

In Mexico, Rosaria used to ride to the clinic high up in the cab of the pick-up. She sat tucked between her grandson and her sister Catalina. The sticky vinyl seat released its smell of sweat and cigarette butts, and the gasoline fumes made Rosaria light-headed in the morning sun.

Catalina would stay with Rosaria while she waited her turn at the clinic, a squat cinderblock building that sat at the edge of the two-lane road. Clay-colored dust settled along the wooden benches where Rosaria and Catalina waited amongst the fishermen, their faces creased with the same clay-colored dust. Older sisters shushed their crying siblings. After Rosaria saw the doctor, Catalina would unpack a basket of warm tortillas, spicy chicken, and beans for them to share.

Now a man younger than her son, with skin dark and smooth like the wooden figures of saints, has come to help Rosaria into a wheelchair. The man is tall, broad-chested in a cotton shirt and trousers the color of dried cockscomb. This, Rosaria knows, is the same uniform worn by the dark, slim girl who brings the food tray and the round one who mops the floor. The man's hair, row upon row of tiny braids, is pulled back from his face and gathered at the nape of his neck, so that a thick rope, like a bundle of fishing net, lies between his shoulder blades.

Rosaria remembers Manzanillo and its wharfs with huts where the women sold whatever fish the men brought in that day. Sometimes there were snapper, sometimes flying fish, and sometimes langostino. The tide lapped at her feet as one of the women wrapped her purchase in brown paper, and the sun hung low in the sky.

The man with hair like a fishing net smiles at Rosaria. His gray eyes reassure her before he lifts her like a feather pillow into the wheelchair. Rosaria knows what will happen now; Luz and Umberto have explained it. Like the last time, the medicine will make Rosaria weak, and her hair will come out in clumps like chicken feathers. She will be sick. She will not even be able to keep down the broth that Luz brings in a silver thermos.

Hours later, after the poison has run through her body, the man with his hair in ropes helps Rosaria to sit up. He lifts her once again into the wheelchair, tucks a thin blanket around her shoulders and folds another over her legs. The sterile smell clings to her.

Back in the room that she shares with a woman too frail to leave her bed, he presses a rosary—his gift to her—into Rosaria's hand and closes her fingers around the cool crystal beads. A blessing before *La Divinia Providencia*, she thinks.

Rosaria remembers that it was here in this hospital that she'd met her first granddaughter. Umberto pushed her in the wheel chair, through long halls with many people rushing past, to the small room on the other side of the hospital. There, Luz lay, resting against fresh pillows. Luz was smiling as she held the fat, healthy baby out to Rosaria. "*Su abuelita*," she whispered. Rosaria touched her lips to the baby's eyelids and cheeks, to her dimpled wrists and her toes.

Now, Luz helps Rosaria to gather her clothing and the small bottles of shampoo and lotion from the set of metal drawers next to the bed. Rosaria wraps the stone figure of *La Virgen* in a square of soft white cloth and tucks it into a plastic shopping bag. She feels for the loop of ribbon she has laced through *La Niña*, presses the warmth of the metal to her skin. She whispers a prayer of thanks for the new baby she will love, for *los milagros* big and small.

MERCY

ONCE, I USED TO CARE ABOUT LOST BOYS

Once, some schoolboys shoved my little brother to the
ground and stuffed his mouth with dirt. I cried and kicked and
fought them and they laughed.

Once, my mother said Aunt Esther was never the same after she'd
lost her son. As a child, I wondered how a mother could be so
careless.

Once, I saw my friend's son sitting on a bench, eating a PB & J
sandwich and gazing out at the river. I waved but he didn't see me. I
looked away.

Once, after my father died, I didn't speak to my brother for
six years.

Once, I saw a homeless boy with straw-colored hair
panhandling in the Acme parking lot. I asked my mother if he
could sleep on our couch for the night and she said yes. In
the morning he was gone.

Once, in tenth grade, my boyfriend raped me in the
guardhouse at the lake where we swam that summer. Later, I
tied his flannel shirt around my waist to hide the bloodstains
on my white Levis.

Once, a couple years later, that same boy had a nervous breakdown
and I felt sad.

Once, my brother climbed up on the roof of our house and
threatened to jump.

Once, my parents took him to a psychologist.

Once, I saw my friend's son peeing in the rain on the side of a
shed, just down the street from their house.

Once, my nephew ate whatever my sister put on his plate.

Once, in seventh grade, my brother got his girlfriend pregnant and she had a late-term abortion. Later, that same girlfriend married another guy and he knocked out her two front teeth.

Once, my friend's son drove his car onto the front porch of a neighbor's house when he was high on oxycodone. Two days later, the mental health clinic discharged him.

Once, my brother ate nothing but chocolate Carnation Instant Breakfast powder straight from the canister all summer long.

Once, my nephew washed his hands eighty-six times in one day.

Once, my brother beat up his second wife and the cops came.

Once, my friend's son spent a couple nights in the county jail.

Once, my friend prayed that her son would find salvation.

Once, my nephew weighed ninety-three pounds his freshman year of college.

Once, I married a boy with a trailer trash mom and no dad. Later, that boy punched a hole through our bedroom wall.

Once, when my friend asked me to talk some sense into her son, the boy's eyes were empty.

Once, I read stories to little boys at a homeless shelter. Their eyes held that same kind of empty.

Once, my brother changed his name.

Once, my brother didn't speak to his son for twenty-three years.

Once, my sister asked me to talk some sense into her son. Once, that same boy told me he danced on the edge of death.

Once, a boy in my third-grade class pushed me down on the playground and a pebble broke the skin of my right knee.

Years later, the scar still shows.

NEST

i

In a dream my mother comes to me as a small bird. After my father's decline, his undignified death, she is clothed in the downy feathers of a fledgling. She darts from windowsill to ceiling, from scratched-dirt floor to tree limb, skeletoned of leaves or berries or blossoms. The bark stripped smooth with no place to nest. This outside-in room, sealed tight as a coffin. She swoops and dips and skitters, her path erratic as that long-ago marriage.

ii

Her wings flap hard at the glass. Does she see her reflection there? A 1950s housewife. Bobby socks, pixie haircut. Just a hair's breadth past childhood and corralled. Brick ranch house and two toddlers: me, my brother. Our father: back from the war, handsome and silent and angry.

iii

A young girl and then an older one, I'd wake to my mother's words. Night after night they slashed the felted darkness, my father's baritone leaden with unspent pain. Years passed and two more siblings arrived. My mother roosted. She flew. She returned. They parted ways, came together decades later. Companions.

iv

Now she tires, rests, tires, rests. My mother's paled feathers float on the draft till they settle to the dust below. And when her strength returns, she flies at the window with all she can muster, her caged fury sharp as the splinters of glass that pierce her avian heart.

LOST SOUL'S JOURNEY

Here in the hospital, they tell me I am dead. The only thing that separates this statement from the *real truth* is a technicality: I don't believe them. When they come, it is hard to know what is real and what is not. There are so many things happening all at once. The voices each fighting for my attention. Some scold me and some plead for mercy.

In the room with blue, padded walls and a lock that scrapes quickly into place, there is plenty of time to sort this out. When they quiet down a bit, I can send them all away and then when the man with sad eyes comes back for me I have stopped screaming.

He sits down beside me on the floor that is covered with blue padding, too. He sits beside me and touches my hand gently.

"Are you ready, Julia?" he asks.

"Yes," I tell him.

"How are you feeling now?" he asks.

I want to yell at him, but then I see behind the thick lenses of his glasses the brownish circles, like two puddles, beneath his eyes. I imagine he must be very tired, watching over people like me all the time.

"They're quiet now," I tell him.

"Good, Julia, that's good. It means the medication is working."

I know that I can trust him, but not the others.

○

I remember, many years ago, seeing Julia at my Aunt Mitzi's house for Rosh Hashanah dinner. I was twenty-eight then and Julia thirty. The rest of us, of course, were all dressed somberly—appropriately—in fall clothing. The Jewish holidays had always imposed what I thought a rather abrupt end to summer, and so I felt childishly resentful and even, I admit, a bit jealous when I saw Julia. She was wearing a white, gauzy skirt and a pale green, sleeveless blouse. She had on those lace-up sandals that were in style that summer. The straps crisscrossed her narrow ankles and the thin soles slapped on my aunt's tile floor as she walked. A pair of beaded, silver earrings swayed against her cheeks each time she turned her head, and dozens of silver bracelets clinked against one another on her bare, tanned arms.

Julia stood frozen for a long moment in the foyer, and I saw the way her eyes darted around the room like a caged animal; she seemed, already, to be planning her escape.

She saw me then, and flitted across the wide foyer with her arms outspread. I had not seen Julia in three years, not since her mother's funeral.

"Look at you!" she said in a voice much louder than anyone's in the house. "You're pregnant, Lorraine!"

"I know," I laughed. "I certainly am."

"How does it feel?" She placed her hand eagerly on my enormous belly and I didn't move, but waited several moments until she backed away, embarrassed and now flustered.

"It feels fine," I said. "That's okay., really. Lots of people do that."

"But, I shouldn't have touched...I could have hurt it."

"Don't be silly, Julia. How are you? How is your father? I haven't seen him in such a long time."

"He's married now," she said dismissively.

Julia tugged at several strands of her corn silk-blond hair, cut stylishly into a long shag. I felt dowdy and rotund in my maternity clothes—a dark blue suit with a stretch panel sewn into the front of the skirt and a pair of sensible loafers, the only shoes that still fit my swollen feet.

"Oh," I said. "I didn't know that. He must have been so lonely when your mother died. I guess..."

"I hate her. She's awful!"

Julia tugged at her hair more urgently and I grew anxious watching her.

"How is Carlton?" I asked meekly, not knowing how to retreat from a subject that was obviously so disturbing to Julia.

In that moment, her eyes softened and she looked, for the first time since we'd been talking, directly at me.

"He takes care of me, you know. He's the best brother anyone could have."

"I did know that, Julia. I know how close you and Carlton have always been. That's nice that you still are."

I now knew how Julia had gotten herself to our aunt's house; Carlton had dropped her off and would come back later to fetch her. He was two years younger than Julia. He hadn't spoken a word to any of us since his mother's death.

Three years earlier I'd embraced Carlton in the malignant stillness of the funeral home. Slight, but appearing even smaller then, engulfed in a dark, wrinkled suit that looked borrowed, he stood rigidly, his body deflecting my inept attempt to comfort him. I could feel his breastbone pressing against my chest, and

33

I'd thought then of the baby bird that Carlton had nursed back to health in a shoebox when we were children. We could see the heart pulsing weakly and the outline of each tiny bone beneath the bird's pink flesh. Carlton dutifully fed the creature with a medicine dropper until it was well enough to fly.

Behind him, my Aunt Roslyn lay against the pale, rose-colored satin of her casket. Julia had been hospitalized again but, had the situation been otherwise, Carlton would never have allowed Julia to see her mother as she was at the end. My aunt's once-plump body had become decimated throughout the months of her illness. My mother had come home from her sister's hospital room tearful and exhausted. "Roslyn's so tiny now," she'd cried into my father's shoulder. "There's almost nothing left of her." And when the funeral director slowly closed the heavy lid of the casket after we said goodbye and before the start of the service, I imagined my Aunt Roslyn had grown as tiny as Carlton's baby bird.

By then, he had refused our family's society entirely; there was a deep resentment on his part. In his opinion, we had all abandoned Julia, but no one so much as their father. My uncle put the house up for sale just a few weeks after my aunt's diagnosis of Hodgkin's Disease, and a few months after her death he'd moved himself into a small condo across town. According to my aunts, he had a "lady friend" then with whom he spent a great deal of time. Julia was to live in a group home, where Carlton, I learned, came down to visit each weekend from Harvard, where he was teaching then.

At my Aunt Mitzi's I remember thinking how beautiful Julia looked then, lithe and ethereal, but clinging only tenuously to what I then thought of as sanity.

I have a lot of shoes. If there's one thing my mother taught me, it's that the right pair of shoes can *make* the outfit. So, this is why I always splurge on shoes. My red cowboy boots are, by far, the ones I love the most. I have a tiny foot so I was lucky to find them in size five, on clearance at Lord & Taylor. Of course, I had to look a long time before I found them. But once I did, I knew I had to have them. They come about halfway up my calf and the stitching swirls around to trace the pattern of a leaf that goes all the way up the front. If I wear them without hose, I can feel the pattern on my skin, just scratchy enough to let me know it's there. Like the plastic bracelet the man with sad eyes put onto my wrist when I was admitted to the hospital.

Julia is two years older than me; when we were children I worshipped her for this, and for her silky, blond hair and the collection of porcelain dolls that lined her room. Each doll sat primly, one next to the other, on shelves Julia was expected to dust each Sunday. Julia was generous with her things and, even though she was often quiet and brooding, I liked spending time with her. She wasn't clingy like many girls, but self-contained, content to sit silently and press her Colorform *people onto one of several cheerful backdrops while I played, unimpeded, with Julia's stock of well-outfitted* Barbies.

From Julia's room, I could hear my mother and Julia's mother—Aunt Roslyn—laughing and talking in the kitchen, and I can remember several years like this of unmarred calm that now fills a dimly lit though pleasant corner of my childhood.

But when Julia was fourteen and I was twelve, everything changed. Now Aunt Roslyn and my mother talked only in whispers when Julia and I came into the kitchen. What little I did overhear made no sense to me. My aunt and uncle spoke to my mother in a language of euphemisms that my child's vocabulary had yet to decipher: Julia was "not right." Julia "could do with a good, long rest."

It was then I surmised that my cousin was suffering an unnamed though apparently dire illness. Why else would her parents be sending her to the hospital?

When I am not here, in the hospital, I go back and forth to Burwood by train. We live in the city now, Carlton and I, but Burwood is where we grew up. This is where our *real* house is. Only it's not our house anymore, not since our mother died.

Carlton says to be careful. When I get back to the train station in the city, it's dirty, not like the station at Burwood where I can sit most of the day. In the city, there are millions of people rushing to their jobs in big office buildings. The people on the train carry lots of bags. Some have nice leather briefcases. The younger ones wear headphones and carry a *Walkman* in one hand. They wear backpacks. I can hear their music sometimes, and their songs are angry. Those songs are constantly mocking me with their angry words.

A lot of nurses and doctors ride the train. Some wear the blue cotton scrubs and some wear the green ones. They each wear a nametag that hangs from a cord around their neck or it clips to their pocket. Carlton says there are good hospitals in the city.

Some of the women carry sturdy canvas bags with their initials stitched on the front. They have books they like to read on the train. The men read the newspaper. Some type on a computer or talk on their phones. They try hard not to look at me.

There were times I can remember feeling like I was nearly as crazy as Julia. This was before the Prozac, when a heaviness like wet cement sucked me down for three or four days at a time before I wrenched myself free again. I thought that perhaps we had each inherited the seeds for insanity and, only by chance, my affliction had taken a somewhat milder, more slowly progressive form.

When Julia was diagnosed with schizophrenia, I had yet to encounter the first pangs of depression, a word I hadn't even learned until I'd gone back to nursing school after the divorce. I was thirty when I signed the papers I thought would free me. Our daughter Maddie was only two. I'd known right from the start that Paul and I wouldn't work, but I was so needy then, and I'd clung to the hope—well beyond the point of reason—that the marriage would somehow "fix" me.

But the first real hints of depression surfaced while I was still in high school. I know this only now. I remember, one night, staring at the purple flowers of my bedroom wallpaper, spinning and nauseous, still tasting vomit and the sweet wine that had induced it. I was crying, I thought then, for the Vietnam vet who gazed for hours at the mall parking lot from his wheel chair and for the POWs and the MIAs for whom my fourth-grade class had worn bracelets with their names inscribed. I also cried for the children with their starved, distended bellies in Bangladesh that were all over the front pages of the newspaper for a while. I cried for all of this or none of this, but I remember feeling at seventeen as though I might shatter to bits.

Julia's illness, of course, had become much more difficult to hide, and it symptoms seeped out against even her parents' will, their daughter's insanity a weeping and ugly stigmata. Julia mumbled incessantly to herself or shouted angrily at demons only she could hear taunting her. While my aunt and uncle tried to silence Julia's outbursts—out of shame or heartbreak, I was never certain—it was always Carlton who gently led her back from the dark passages through which she had begun to wander more frequently then.

Julia and Carlton always had a quiet but fierce sibling loyalty that I, an only child, envied and sometimes resented. But I realize now, too, they'd been bound to one another not just by the tether of familial love, but by an even deeper instinct to survive. Carlton had been gentle and timid as a boy, and it was this perhaps, and his uncanny brilliance—apparent even in grade school—that separated him so distinctly from his classmates. Carlton and I were in the same grade, and I knew, as children do, that the bullies had marked him.

One afternoon at the beginning of our fourth-grade school year, Carlton and I waited for Julia outside the doors of the upper school. Julia was in sixth grade then and we were all to walk home together. It had grown chilly and Carlton pulled his blue knit cap down further over his ears. The cap framed his small, angular face, pulling his eyebrows down into the impression of a sad clown.

Julia was late coming out and the schoolyard was nearly empty. We walked silently past the ball fields and headed out along the chain-link fence that surrounded the school. Suddenly, three older boys, boys in Julia's grade, crowded in around us. They took turns ramming into Carlton, pushing him from side to side until he lost his balance and fell to the sidewalk. One of the boys, heavy-set with wiry, red hair, yanked Carlton's blue cap from his head.

"Give it back," Carlton said, reaching for his hat.

"Whatsa matter, faggot," the boy whined, "Ya need your big retard sister to walk you home?"

I tasted fear at the back of my throat and knew with a sickening awareness that I was powerless to move.

The other two boys hung back, but the big one dragged Carlton from the sidewalk and threw him down onto the muddy embankment bordering the schoolyard. He rolled Carlton onto his stomach and pressed his face into the ground with his knee.

"Hey, Carrrl-ton," the redhead whined, "How 'bout tastin' some nice dirt! That's what you faggot boys like isn't it?"

Carlton was crying then, heavy sobs that sounded like choking.

I remember that I was shouting and my own voice frightened me. I heard then, too, what seemed an unending and savage shriek, one solid tone of hatred that kept pace with my heartbeat. I remember that Julia's face was scarlet, her blond hair flying out wildly, and then she was upon the bully, kicking his ribs with her saddle shoes, and next sinking her teeth into his cheek as he tried, too late, to cover his face with his flailing arms.

"Get off me, you freak!"

But the boy's voice was gravelly with tears as he shook Julia loose. An impression of Julia's teeth stood out in purpling blood on the boy's freckled skin.

Bits of grass and dirt clung to Carlton's tear-streaked face as we walked home amid the autumn scent of rotting leaves.

It would take me many years to understand how far Julia had strayed from all of us. By then I'd begun therapy in earnest, at first only an afterthought when Paul stormed out of our last marriage counseling session. I had learned the name for what was wrong with me, but not how to assuage the niggling feelings of sorrow that chewed incessantly at the edges of my thoughts.

I remember how my mother's greenhouse smelled. The air inside was thick and moist. I could feel droplets of water on my skin. I could hear the little fans whirring. The air smelled like dirt and the little pebbles that lay in the bottom of the orchid trays. There was a pungent, acid smell too that I could almost taste on my tongue. That was the fertilizer, she told me. But then there was Jasmine and Plumeria that smelled so sweet it made me dizzy. My mother let me touch their petals and they felt like velvet. This was when I was very little. This was a long time before my mother died.

On my way to work at the hospital, there was always a man curled up, sleeping on the metal grate. I would see him walking across campus sometimes. He looked straight down at his feet the whole time he was walking. He ate what he found in the trashcans or what the vendors had given him that day. When he slept, he kept his boots—in a clear plastic bag—under his head for a pillow. This still wasn't as bad, I thought, as the woman who slept—with her shopping cart, and bags and bags of things piled about her—against the bus stop glass. One time it almost broke my heart; she had a child with her then. It was early in the morning, even before the rush of commuters streamed from the train station and to their jobs in the city. I thought about Julia then. I thought that if it hadn't been for Carlton, this, too, could be Julia.

I went to college one year. I'm just as smart as anyone, Carlton told me. It was cold a lot and very gray in Syracuse that autumn. My parents visited on family weekend and Carlton drove up from Burwood a few times in a dented *Pinto* he said he'd borrowed from a friend. Once, my cousin Lorraine came to see me. But when the demons returned, I never went back. I never went back after they came to me at school; they'd found me even there.

The best thing that came of my short-lived marriage was Maddie. And the best thing that came of the divorce was Ellie, the therapist I inherited after Paul and I had given up on marriage counseling. She was a kind, middle-aged Jewish woman who coaxed me through a period so miserable I truly believed I would not emerge whole. Ellie helped me to begin what would turn out to be a lifelong task. Then, too, it had become easier for me to spend time again with Julia. I wasn't quite as frightened of her anymore. Or, perhaps, I was no longer frightened that I would slip, imperceptibly, into a world that looked more like Julia's than my own.

For a while, though, she'd been doing better. She was taking her medication again, a new one. She had a small apartment, and a boyfriend—a pale, anemic-looking guy with wispy, brown hair and kind eyes —who sometimes lived there with Julia. Her father, of course, must have paid the bills; Julia had never worked.

I hadn't expected Julia's apartment to be tidy, but neither had I been prepared for the magnitude of disarray. I remember first sitting at the tiny kitchen table, still covered with crumbs and sticky with jam from Julia's breakfast. Dirty dishes and cups were piled in the sink and on a small, makeshift counter. A plastic ashtray overflowed with cigarette butts and the air was foul with smoke. When I excused myself to use the bathroom, I found the bathtub filled with soiled laundry and stacks of newspaper and magazines. The stacks hovered at the rim of the tub; some went even higher.

"Oh, that," said Julia when I asked her if she needed some help cleaning up. "I've been thinking about that. Carlton helped me last time."

I could feel Julia's chaos pressing in around me, and I found myself breathing in a shallow, rapid way that made me feel like I was drowning. The task of separating what was to be discarded and what to be saved seemed daunting then. Julia had no hamper and no laundry basket, so I tossed a mounting pile of damp and dirty clothing, sheets, and towels into the hallway. Later, I thought, I

39

would take Julia to the K-Mart and buy her some essentials. As we worked, Julia periodically drifted off into the kitchen with an old TV Guide *or* Mademoiselle *we had discarded only moments before.*

I don't know why this experience had shaken me so, but I left Julia that afternoon feeling exhausted and hopeless. I thought of the glowing ashes of Julia's endless cigarettes igniting piles of newspaper, of the gas jets of the rusting stove hissing their poison into Julia's sleeping body. And I thought of the thin girl they'd wheeled in through the trauma bay who had succeeded at what Julia, in worse times, had attempted herself.

Carlton said not to turn on the TV. Something bad happened, he said. Something terrible. I saw it anyway. I saw the way the plane crashed right into the building, again and again. Right in the middle of the city where people work. I saw the fire exploding in the sky. I saw how scared those people were. Some of them were running and some of them couldn't even walk because they were hurt. There was so much smoke, and those people looked like ghosts. I can still see them when I close my eyes. They were gray like ghosts. Carlton said not to watch anymore. Then Carlton said it was time to come back to the hospital, to the man with sad eyes.

I remember when I began to see Julia at the train station. By then, she had deteriorated drastically. I knew she'd been hospitalized again, just after the terrorist attacks. I knew that Carlton had then moved her into his apartment in the city, and that he'd hired a nurse to care for Julia while he worked. He'd left Harvard and accepted a professorship at Penn so that he could be close to Julia again.

I'd been struggling then, too. The 9/11 attacks triggered a drowning sadness in me and a whole host of new fears. I couldn't bring myself to face Julia in the hospital then. Things had fallen apart between Aaron, my second husband, and me, and we were civil to one another only so long as my daughter Maddie was in the room. My second marriage seemed as hopeless as the first. I felt I had no place left to go that was safe.

40

It was then that Julia had begun to appear like an apparition visible only to me. I worked the night shift in the Emergency Department, and coming down the steps to the train tracks in the still-dark morning, I often felt like a sleepwalker, moving only under the power of frayed nerves and the adrenaline high from our last case.

One raw, winter morning, I saw Julia, perched tentatively on the steps leading down to the platform. The solemn parade of shift workers veered only slightly to avoid her. She was wearing deep red lipstick that was stark against her leathered face. Strands of her hair—now graying like mine—escaped a thin cotton shawl she'd draped over her head and shoulders. She had no coat and no gloves. She clasped a slim, black handbag to her breasts, and I noticed that she had on white pants, terribly soiled, that were stuffed into the tops of a pair of red cowboy boots.

Looking at Julia's face, I saw how immeasurably she had aged since I'd seen her last. A network of deep lines was now etched into her once-smooth skin. She was only forty-five, but the leathery skin of her face and hands was that of an old woman's. As I approached her, Julia's eyes were at once frantic and defiant. She looked at me for what seemed a long time; then, without speaking, she clattered back up the steps just as the train that would deliver me to the suburbs screeched to a stop.

When we were little, my brother Carlton and I sledded down the hill behind our house. All the kids from our neighborhood would come because it was the best hill for sledding. There were trails that took you to the lake. If you knew how to steer through the trees and you didn't fall off, you could glide right out onto the ice. You had to lean real hard to the right when Carlton did. And the tighter you squeezed with your arms around his waist and your knees bent and pressing against his ribs, the faster you would go. Then you tasted the pellets of wooly snow on Carlton's blue hat and let them melt on your tongue.

I remember that the TV was never off. We watched CNN in the family waiting room, in the lounge, and then at home, later, I couldn't take my eyes off of it. I'd worked a double shift. No one knew what would happen next. We followed the disaster plan, the trauma team at full capacity.

Now a full year later, after 9-11, when I got off the train, I looked up at the sky and instead of cloudless blue, I saw airplanes crashing, a mushroom cloud of black smoke, sharp, orange flames, unholy and merciless. I saw buildings toppling and people crying and stumbling. Their faces and clothing were covered in ash. I saw people flying, on fire, from buildings. They were ghosts, flying like angels into a sky I no longer recognized.

Aaron and I were working hard to stay together, to be there for Maddie. I was still frightened a lot. I wondered if the windows in the train station were bomb-proof, and I asked my doctor to increase my dosage of Prozac. I was holding on, but only barely.

I knew how it would be. They had been telling me for so long that I memorized it like a prayer. Death is like that; it's familiar and, in a funny way, it's like a warm, safe spot to rest.

I've been so tired. I was tired of running from them always. They turned me ugly, too, with their vicious words, their brutal stares. The eyes of demons.

And when they're quiet, only a whisper, they tell me how to hold the plastic tight against my face. They tell me how the air inside my lungs will burn hot at first and I will feel like I am drowning. But soon I am flying, my arms outspread and when the sun touches my face, it is like soft fingers stroking my cheek. I am resting now, and the man with sad eyes is watching me.

When Carlton called, I knew before the phone rang what he would say. On that first-year anniversary perhaps Julia, too, had been revisited by specters that flew, again and again, from the burning towers, saddened ghosts hovering so close she could touch them. I was sick with grief and with guilt and, still, I could not see her face.

But then at my Aunt Mitzi's, there among the trays of cold cuts and the plates mounded with sweets, and the younger children being hushed by my cousins, I imagined Julia. She was beckoning me then, her silver bracelets tinkling against one another as she walked. She, alone had crossed the threshold, and I had remained behind.

The rabbis tell us that suicide is the most horrific sin, unforgivable; one life taken is like the taking of all. I saw Julia's soul wandering then, as she had in the morning hours, through the rank station, between the realm of the living and what comes after.

I was angry with God—for his impotence, his disinterest—as Julia and I had each made our choices. But I prayed that night anyway, for the first time in a very long time, and I asked God to watch over Julia. To watch over us all.

ANGELS AMONG US

INCREMENTS

The old man
rakes leaves
into tiny piles
I cannot fathom.
He skirts the little birdbath,
the purple and russet pansies
a good deal of effort
and something gentle
in each step.

Tiny piles
increments
so close to one another
like patience,
and bundled carefully

in moments
or years
gathered and waiting
within the tidy white fence.

And I
rushing by
each day
seeing him smile
from beneath his woolen cap
measuring
my frantic progress
by where he stands.

FIRSTBORN

Selengei had chosen the name during the wet season, many months before. This one was to be a daughter. She would call her Adia, a gift from *Ngai*—for this baby would be a precious gift, her first-born. Already fourteen, Selengei had attended many births and yearned for the time her own baby would suckle at her breast.

Now as she felt the insistence of her unborn baby's head, Selengei knew she must push harder. Down, down, down! Her mouth stretched wide, tusks arcing to the heavens. Only *Ngai* would hear Selengei's silent screams from atop his mountain throne. She thought of nothing then—not of the others who stood and soothed her— only of her baby. She pushed again and her birth water rushed out like the great river Karura. The swill of water and blood washed over her feet as she stepped carefully over her baby. The girl-calf lay curled and silent against the earth.

Selengei prodded the infant, first gently with the fingers of her trunk, listening for the breath. She pressed one foot to the baby's shoulder, rocked her, and then—as she knew she must—began to kick, harder, then harder still. If her baby did not stand, she could not suckle. Selengei's heart surged with anguish. Tears slipped down her wrinkled face. The others drew closer. Selengei slipped her trunk under the baby's head and lifted the sweet face toward her own. She kicked at the dry-season dust. She kicked, and the others—daughters, sisters, aunts, mothers, and grandmothers—kicked until all were certain. Until the baby Adia lay covered in dust.

Selengei's baby was stillborn and so her sorrow swelled and churned. Again, she remembered the river, Grandmother Rukiya leading the herd across the shallows, Selengei's mother—then the others— coaxing baby Selengei on that very first crossing. Then year after year, Grandmother leading them further, further, beyond the crashing falls.

Now Selengei held the infant closer. As she lifted her gift to Ngai, Selengei wept, her keening rising, rising along with the others', until the swollen river spilled.

TOWARD THE LIGHT

PRACTICUM

My daughter's chin
fits perfectly
within
my cupped hand.

I hold her
like this
feeling
the finite edge
of this geometry
where her bony angles
meet the triangle
I make of my palm

and fitting snugly
my daughter resting here with me
the proof to this equation
floats beyond my grasp of mathematics
of everything they could not teach me.

HISTORICAL NOTE

On March 11–13, 1938, Nazi Germany annexed the neighboring country of Austria. This event, known as the *Anschluss*, a German word that means "connection" or "joining," was a harbinger of the horrors to come. In the wake of the *Anschluss*, Austrians persecuted the country's Jewish population. Between this time and the outbreak of World War II in 1941, some 300,000 Jews escaped Austria, Germany, and Czechoslovakia, finding refuge in such places as the Bosnian cities of Brčko, Bijeljina, and Sarajevo.

However, their escape was short-lived. In western Yugoslavia, the Holocaust was carried out by the *Ustaše*, a brutal Nazi puppet regime that decimated Bosnia's Jewish community. The *Ustaše* movement in Brčko initiated a wave of terror against local Serbs and Jews that went even beyond the terror policies introduced by the central Independent State of Croatia (NDH) authorities.

Throughout Bosnia and Croatia, the regime extinguished the lives of between 12,000 and 20,000 Jews; between 320,000 and 340,000 ethnic Serbs; between 15,000 and 20,000 Roma (Gypsies); and between 5,000 and 12,000 ethnic Croats and Muslims, who were political opponents of the regime.

The woman depicted in "Strong Swimmer" is a fictional character. However, she represents one of 350 Jews imprisoned, tortured, and murdered in Brčko, over the course of two December days in 1941.

ACKNOWLEDGMENTS

"In Times Like These" *Zin Daily*. October 2024

"Ghusl" *Zin Daily*. October 2023

"Far from Home" *Chautauqua*. June 2024

"Strong Swimmer" and "Not Ours" *Unbroken*. July 2023

"Prayer for a Pandemic" *Please See Me*. July 2020

"All that We Hear *en Los Estados Unidos" Chronogram*. June 2020

"After Florence, Rooftop Stigmata" *Split Rock Review*. March 2019

"Boy, Bearing" *Medical Literary Messenger*. January 2019

"Once, I Used to Care about Lost Boys" *Pembroke Magazine*. Spring 2019

"Nest" *Thrice Fiction*. April 2018

"Setting Anchor" *Wilderness House Literary Review*. Summer 2017

"Firstborn" *Lime Hawk*. March 2017

"Los Milagros" *Lalitamba*. October 2006

"Lost Soul's Journey" *Bellevue Literary Review*. Fall 2006

"Increments" *Journal of Pastoral Care and Counseling*. Fall 2006

"Practicum" *Chronogram*. November 2005

I would like to express my gratitude to the late Philip Gerard, Malena Mörling, Gregory Djanikian, and James Rahn for their guidance, generosity, and support. Special thanks to Jill Gerard, Diane Sorenson, and Doug Hansen—each have contributed considerable talent, love, and friendship to this project. I am grateful to Alan Abrams at Sligo Creek Publishing for finding beauty between the jagged lines of pain. Many thanks to Natalija Grgorinić and Ognjen Rađen for providing blessed space and time at the Zvona I Nari Cultural Center in Istria, Croatia. Finally, to my husband and enduring partner Robert Greenberg: none of this is possible without you.

BIOGRAPHY

DINA GREENBERG

Nominated for The Pushcart Prize, Best Small Fictions, and The Millions, Dina Greenberg's cross-genre works have appeared in literary journals and media outlets throughout the U.S. and internationally. Her debut novel *Nermina's Chance* received the first place 2022 Firebird Award in literary fiction. Ms. Greenberg holds an MFA from the University of North Carolina Wilmington, where she served as managing editor for the literary journal *Chautauqua*. She leads creative writing workshops across academic, nonprofit, and community-based settings.

www.ingramcontent.com/pod-product-compliance
Lightning Source LLC
Chambersburg PA
CBHW040852120626
46547CB00006B/586